T0049083

Soft Inheritance

soft inheritance

Fawn Parker

Palimpsest Press
1171 Eastlawn Ave.
Windsor, Ontario. N8S 3J1
www.palimpsestpress.ca

Printed and bound in Canada
Cover design and book typography by Ellie Hastings
Edited by Jim Johnstone

Palimpsest Press would like to thank the Canada Council for the Arts
and the Ontario Arts Council for their support of our publishing
program. We also acknowledge the assistance of the Government of
Ontario through the Ontario Book Publishing Tax Credit.

LIBRARY AND ARCHIVES CANADA CATALOGUING IN PUBLICATION

TITLE: Soft inheritance / Fawn Parker.
NAMES: Parker, Fawn, 1994- author.
DESCRIPTION: Poems.
IDENTIFIERS: Canadiana (print) 2023048896X
            Canadiana (ebook) 20230488978

ISBN 9781990293528 (SOFTCOVER)
ISBN 9781990293535 (EPUB)
CLASSIFICATION: LCC PS8631.A7535 S64 2023 | DDC C811/.6—DC23

For E.

Contents

3

4

1

GAVAGE

First I replaced the head, then the handle,
then it was not my grandfather's axe.

I used the blade to shave the soft down
and my wrist flicked: a familial trick.

I wrapped a white flag around
my ass and pissed into it.

They found me in the room among my parts:
pieces of Theseus' ship,

decorated with images of apples
and snakes, soaked with urine.

There was a paper trail,
a maze made to be completed by an idiot,

a maze made of corn, boiled with fat,
and worked through a tube.

On the walls hung photographs
of the men in our families.

The doctor let me steady his hand.
This way I was provided the illusion of control.

An overfed goose,
boiled in can, and sold as novelty.

The blunt end of the tool dented the lid and secured it.
Preserved until displayed, in patience.

FASTING FOR GOD

I was introduced to the idea of starvation
at the mercy of men by my mother

Walking into the parting crowd
she pointed and said,

"He loves you, he loves you."
When she's wrong I blame the men

The way they stomp their boots on asphalt,
on porch steps, in the basement

Into the precious diorama my horned father
built to cage my small, small mother

I'm presented with the microphone
asked: what is it called if you get the worst hand possible

My mother, beat-less, says, marriage!
and laughs. She embellishes

each time, she embellishes.

THE MORNING AFTER ROKY PLAYED LEE'S

The rest of us have
demons too—

first like a child,
then like a husband

reborn or born-again,
become the artist

who gave me
a discount on the heart

tattooed on my arm.
He crawled down

from my attic room,
and released himself.

A roach under a beam,
black dots in a line

down his forehead
the watchful eyes of God

POEM AGAINST MY HUSBAND

My husband says there is one place I can't
do it and I do it there

I don't come, and I don't want to
so instead I write couplets.

I am lonely and the thought
of others makes me sick

at least in the mornings.
By night I'm in need again.

I stink of salt rock deodorant
and my hand is chafed

from the chain around another neck
I only pretended I wanted it

because I needed momentum
The rock up the hill, et cetera

But for the love of things
I do nothing.

My work needs me like an infant—
this is why we understand each other.

ABRACADABRA
For Joshua Chris Bouchard

There were times you didn't understand:
goodness is a scar.

Outside, but inside too.
The fenced-in patio.

We laugh until we twist
in horror and withdraw.

If you go to the party there will be someone there
who takes it out of you.

You want something from the party,
but the party is a beast

and you are speaking to some part of it
that isn't its ear.

Your calls come through in silence
and I am somewhere else—

ocean in a conch,
blood in the cochlea,

in some combination there is an anagram
that benefits everyone.

I am not a person deserving of a word
like light.

ANIMAL OF CHOICE

I've rented a 1½ with heating issues and a rule against dogs. I project death where it doesn't belong: won't I be gone before the lease is up anyway? I overlook the particulars in favour of being close, thinking at least I can die here, too. I do the same with others—I number friends' days. I weep at their feet. Crawl on all fours as distraction, self-domesticate, become a fixture. I let go of material objects. I replace them with what's in the will. My friends are useless and it's not their fault. I say nothing to them, wait for them to pass me the muzzle. Now I have become the bitch. Now I take my coffee with milk and white sugar.

Of course Nancy will get the car, says my mother, and writes it down.
For me, the ring, and the dog.
The house won't be mine but it's for me to sell.
Where will I put the dog?

I want to tell Klein, but I already have too many strikes with the new girl. Things feel frivolous. The previous arrangement had been that the ring would be resized for when he needed it. He was meant to give it to me—not my mother.

Recently I prayed in the living room at the coffee table. I couldn't remember if the proper way was with my hands clasped or flat together. Soon I will inherit the table, so I can try again.

JOLIE-LAIDE

I want simple things
carefully chosen:

black cotton,
black leather,

gold jewelry on my arms
and a significant finger.

Dr. Kirsch laughs
when I say I look ugly

in the mirrors
in my mother's house.

"Too perfect," we say,
like girlfriends.

I want her like I want
any blonde in brown lipstick.

"Not pretty ugly,"
I say,
"Pretty-ugly."

BAIT AGE

You don't have to be pretty
to be pretty to a man who hates his wife.

I should have settled for unhappy
and unfucked, I realize,

changing the address on my manuscripts.
Now I live alone in my mother's house

and walk between floors with my ears plugged.
Feel her eyes on my stockings,

torn by the man in the white car.
But when I look through the banister rails

her eyes are shut, and tense. She's not there.
I leave when it gets dark and return, still dark.

I photograph the prints on my ass
and address men like professionals.

My mother leans forward in her gown
skin like a boot broke through the ground.

She says, Can I tell you? I hate how I smell now
the yeast-scent of wound

or I imagine it, strength of suggestion.
Nancy is getting the car

you're getting the diamond, I already told you.
She re-tells stories, I forget details.

In my absence
rats come into the house and take the oxy.

The doctors count
and accuse my mother of over-use.

SOFT INHERITANCE

I remember you went ah
ran your hand over

starched white cotton
upright, to protect the port

I hold up options:
off-white, pale blue

You can't remember the colour
of the hospital room

you say, any colour but that.
You've forgotten again:

kindness is a scar
though not all scar-makers are kind

your mastectomy
and my underdeveloped left side

like some sort of punchline.
We are sisters of misery

Tattooed barbed wire mimics
your centipede stitch

I comb through the albums
and throw out the doubles

Drag files into folders,
drag folders into the trash

The paint chips match
the blur of some bluish background

A single zoomed pixel:
a location on your face

I zoom out and the photo is of me,
not you. I am with a man

Without him, I am limp
He goes soft in my hand and I am lonely

I used to feel empty without a man
until I saw a diagram showing

that the cunt is closed,
touching itself, when not in use.

IMPACT

Walking by my mother's room
I mistake her for her wig

She's in the living room
in a baseball cap

Everything is salt to me,
she says,

rejects food
ignores my anecdotes about

men, and jobs
in America

I tell her stop crying,
phone my sister

crying,
saying where are you

why me why not you
I sleep with the photo albums

closed
Lie in her bed and pretend cancer's

spreading into me, too
At night I ask Klein to hit me

Where, he asks
and I gesture to my breast.

TRIPLE NEGATIVE

Why kick the mutt snoring hungrily
when there are men

horny for a heel
in the groin

It's not substitution, I insist
raising out of the armchair

If I fuck in addition
to the grieving

The therapist blinks
I sit still on the bus ride home

Read the weekly forecasts:
today she is in less pain

The humidity swells
her skin under the wraps

I can feel it myself until I go out
The chill wipes the dream from my skin

Wherein I felt the swell, pinched my arm
and was confronted with the distance

The websites say this means
I am ready for a change

I woke up with the mall today
watching the fashion stores blink, and open

I had to get out because I thought
again about a man I gave up on

And I wanted to pass
silently

from Bathurst to Bloor-Yonge,
to Dundas by foot

While my phone flashed on the coffee table

FOUND POEM B SIDE
Live transcription of my mother, January 2019

I have had so many lives

      I sit at my table
      where I do my thinking

and I think

      I am a happy person
      considering

I have my house
my children—one of them—

      my routine

My doctor taught me this:

      "new normal"

I don't live in waiting but yes
I do wait

      This year I turn 64

Some people do just one thing
I do it all

      It's kind of interesting
      I'm even interested

in myself

For example I don't take shit
        from anybody

ST. AGATHA'S PLATTER

Every morning leading up to the marathon
I walked the route
and took the streetcar back
which took me three times as long

It kept me above ground
where first I called my mother,
then my father. If it's unsuccessful, she says,
at least I won't know!

The race? Or the—
My line cuts, anyway.
My father says he'll go to her
but only if she asks

God Bless St. Agatha
for bringing my family back together again

WHAT ARE WE HERE FOR

While my mother waits
for the ambulance
I sit and write

One-handed,
with metal from Italy
Agatha-stamped
in my other

What are we here for?
I hear a man enter the house

Me,
she says

breathless
as if playing

at flirtation
Did I use up her

breath?
Repeating and repeating

her words to myself,
in my notebooks

The men make her climb
the staircase

Now,
she says

Now, it's happening
again

She is wired
to screeching machines

The house is a hospital
a single room
an open cage
a staircase

2

GOLDEN RAYS OF CHEMO

A large left lump
skewing the skin like
a sickle like a stump like a

weak spot in a balloon

The broken latex over shellac
the oil in the ocean
the come
        and go

2017
was the summer
of my mother's breasts

Golden rays of chemo

       washing

chamomile and lemon juice

The dog walker left forbidden fruit
on the kitchen island

Let her have some fun,
she said,
a bird in the hand
is a flat straight line

STRAWBERRY THIEF

(i)

We disagreed,
my mother and I,
though we were both wrong.

I saw it as a precious red gem,
she a black spider.

It was changing,
shrinking,
always,
anyway.

Unless it wasn't. Then we were in trouble.

We used the phrase "100% cancer-free,"
all of us.

The surgeon,
myself,
my mother.

This was our vision.

My mother laughed and applied her makeup.

She talked freely about death.

(ii)

In the mirror in the stranger's bathroom,
I looked like my mother.

There was genetic testing available to determine if I had
"the gene."

If so, this was the situation:
50/50.

I pulled at the fabric over my navel,
baring my breasts to myself.

Snake eyes.

(iii)

You know what Claire Danes said?
said Emilie,
          the actor?

"Acting is the greatest answer to my loneliness."

If I had the gene they would take my uterus.
But what if I conceived quickly before my operation?

The gene,
the gene.

And if I were to pass it on?

At least I wouldn't be lonely.

At least there would be
someone at my breast.

Even if they took those too.

DISTANCE

It was too expensive
I've let the youthful platinum grow out
a gradient of time and chemical
like the paint brushes in my mother's pantry
I locate on the hair
a time before we knew
and attack with shears, style it like her wig.
Last summer my mother painting and repainted
the kitchen, where she's moved the chaise lounge
to eat mashed chicken in applesauce.
I make this concoction, divide it into Ziploc bags.
I eat it too, or I eat nothing.
I'm restricting again.
My mother's surgeon says
she doesn't have enough body fat
for reconstructive surgery
but lateran implant is optional
She calls me to say this
and other, normal things.
Her new boyfriend the produce manager
washes her wigs in the kitchen sink
With shampoo? I say
Spiking myself on a rock on the shore in Nanaimo
Sorry, she says, Are you roaming?
This is expensive.

RANGE LIFE

I thought I saw my mother
kissing Santa Claus:
just the dog on her hind legs.

Another example
of a woman
being sexless.

I am deranged
and my time will come. But—
no more old men.

Instead, an animal
in a leisure suit
so I can settle down.

ALL MY FRAGILE HERBS
for Ali Pinkney

I tend to simple things:
feed the cat three times

each day. Klein has propped up
cilantro, basil, with paperclips

arranged like a jaw.
Small, slanted inward

orthodontically incorrect
a resemblance to mine

I outgrew the fixture
the structure

the counselling.
It made me indignant

like lipstick and heels
with a forced posture.

Pity it didn't work
and no surprise.

The herbs are so weak
They fall from the weight of their heads

They grow quickly, over-ambitious.
Wilt, and then die

I am here one week
before Klein is back from Europe

Ali brings me her new manuscript,
bundled in purple parchment,

wrapped in a chain with a small pendant,
a puzzle piece stamped with

" ST
ENDS"

I imagine the manufacturer
of the necklace may have—

not in error but indifference—
made the pieces so that they

do not align.
So that they may read:

"ST   BE"
"ENDS   FRI" if linked.

At night,
I hang the pendant over Klein's bedpost.

I enjoy the routine of it all
The cat, the notes, the eye dropper

with liquid fertilizer.
The mechanical chew

of the percolator
making the same

sour cup he must have each day
when he does his work.

In a way
this is everything I've ever wanted.

GOING SHOPPING

In one of your journals I find
entries about how I'm unemotional

Not emotional *enough*,
they say, not enough

for you to relate.
In others it's husband,

husband.
Now that you are gone

I cannot learn from my mistakes,
be the good daughter.

Straighten the back, emote
in appropriate contexts.

Lately I don't say a word.
At the funeral service

I read something old,
unaffected and academic

to everyone
you've ever known.

In this way I succeed
in being recognizable to you

should there be something
you-like in the air around the cemetery.

I am costumed in items I found
"shopping" in your closet.

I sit in your coats,
write in your journal:

"How about now?".
And that's that.

LIKE TO MAKE SPRING

Dread spring
limbs like snakes

body
like a snake's

robust greenery
softened middle

clay-like
cursed—curs-èd—
rattle in wrist

wobble compartment
shake dust
grow horizontal

a rhizome
chlorine of pre-(xxx)
spot on borrowed cloth

dread spring.

SMUG AS VENUS

Many pink surfaces
casings of other
women detail of red
backdrop of white

the mother number
the sharing fabrics
the bloated centre

the

to signify
            strange
to outgrow, outlive
un-avian, static

Valentine frill

tissue without boundary is air
fat is a womb reversal
quoi…
qui, moi?

SURNAME, NAME

In my dream last night Marco
was protesting your burial

(as if I didn't think of that).

For a moment
he had our attention.

Littered the cemetery grounds
with flyers, flashy and laser-printed

In my grandiosity
I thought I read your name

thousands of times.
One of those

names made of
two surnames

But the flyer said something else
and actually it said nothing.

I awoke to a pounding at the door
with a jump

but was mistaken.

GHOST

It was the evening of my mother's wake,
and then it was the morning after.

In my great clarity of mind
I decided we should sort things out.

I wanted to see what you'd say
if I said I could forget about the other girl

but you insisted somebody walk me home.
You insisted: No, I love you

as much as ever. But go home.
We'd be leaving early in the morning

and I was the great navigator!
Well, that's all right.

I didn't want to talk about it anyway.
In fact I never want to talk

at all. You insisted you were only thinking
about how you think I am beautiful.

That's when she called you.
You said many things are out of our control.

My mother told me that hate
is like a stone pushed up a mountain.

Another time she told me
that no good thing comes easy.

You came home without a word,
touched me in some careless way.

I rose before six with the sun,
made breakfast, and wept.

We drove to Lake Couchiching,
the warm air from the vents

like a long sad breath.
We didn't talk.

In the cabin, I lay like a stone
and pretended to be dead. You grew bored

with me. I came to life when you left,
sat wondering by the window.

The lake was a trick
of wind and mist.

You, down there, in your windbreaker.
The sheets damp and heavy around my legs.

I resented you for my feelings
for you, how they coloured my experience

of trying to earn a word like grief,
to not succumb to a word like envy.

The emerald stroke of you
by the shore, your head craned down at your phone

for some indeterminate amount of time.

3

THE GRAND INQUISITORIUM
Poem written by AI in response to poem by Fawn Parker

In front of the picture the people
talk about what they feel
and think. Imaginative? Not in any
sense of the word. An inanity.

When I was twenty-one
I was taken to the Grand Inquisitorium.

An enormous place, the most enormous place
in my life up to that moment.

The door had a tiny lock on it.

In the Grand Inquisitorium

I waited for my turn.
Each new person who came
entered the Grand Inquisitorium

and waited to be told
what to think.

THAT FAMOUS NIGHT

There are so many people
a person can be.
It is a mark of inadequacy,
you might argue,
my having imagined some
other
in your place,
from whom I would continue on past
down a busy street
dropping some insignificant belonging
and saying,
oh,
keep it.
Instead I staggered
tipsy
back to the hotel in the dark
with something more
than I'd had when I left
mourning already
that I'd have to leave it
behind.

THEIR SHELLS GET BLEACHED BY THE SUN

Is a still life
interrupted by the bustling of a ladybug
up the curtains' drawstring
still *still?*
In the trenches of the open windows
the insects lie golden and dead,
their spots holding strong,
or only appearing that way by contrast.
All things seem sure of themselves
in contrast to other things.
I watch ladybugs crawl circles around the pane,
the ones still red,
and look only at the window,
never through,
afraid of what I might see
in place of what I want.
In the kitchen in the mornings
I pour coffee into your mug.
Each time I find it in my hands I put it back down,
only to find myself reaching again.
Once I looked inside and there was a bug
moving wildly on its back.
It doesn't work to close the panes;
they find a way in anyway.
They collect in the sills
and their shells are bleached by the sun.
I said I'd never kill them
but there are so many now that I do.

NICOLAS LALOUX, MAGNETIC HILL, BELGIAN MOON, MOOSEHEAD

All of this drinking frees me.
I say what I say and I move on.
Like how you asked that first night

if without the distance, we'd still...?
—yes. We answered quickly.
As if it were something that could

be jinxed. As if I hadn't already tried
to jinx it before. There was a seed
of you, always threatening to do

what a seed can do. There was
the time I was there for real
as hard as it is to believe I ever was...

When you placed some small seed
of something in my palm and told me:
do nothing with this.

There was the first moment
when I looked at you and thought:
there you are.

Do you know about the rhizome?
It grows sideways instead of upward.
Can you finish this one for me?

About how I moved so far away, and that's where I found you?

1986, THE FIELDS COMPANY OF CHICAGO

purchased the rights to Muzak—
this is how I wanted to begin.

Specificity,
I used to think, was a hand trained to thread
any needle;
there were constellations of muscles
waiting in the sky
to be worked.

> A tactic called Stimulus Progression
> is used to increase worker productivity.
> Muzak consists of 15-minute blocks
> increasing in tempo and instrumentation.

> > 1986:
> > Already somewhere you began to work
> > yourself toward and through a point.

> The company began to record with its own orchestra
> the rising,
> worsening 15-minute segments…

You turn off the highway,
tension like a pin
between your lips.
In a parking lot in rural Quebec,
you exit, run and leap through the air,
your arms stretched over your head.

Old husbands watch from the window
of the bilingual slogan-ed diner
where there are speakers pumping
out something neutral, something
felt, looking in
from the outside. I watch you, still
and as if a photograph, before you leap again
into the air.
The sound fades behind
the increasing orchestra of your movement.

IN THE DOCUMENTARY ABOUT THE ENTIRE WORLD

there are things like
mammoths trundling

across a big screen.
Things like made-up lips

in spreads in fashion
editorials. The editorial

process of describing the day
the ticketer at the Dollar Cinema

said,
You have a nice man

there. I apply something red,
assume the posture of something

evolved. Imagining the spectacle
should the light project back on me

LE SWAN DINER-CAFE

The A/C drips and I
imagine blood

I am alone in the booth
waiting for you

I cut a hole in the door
and install a flap

In time you become
unforbidden, unexciting

In time I am arched,
then upright

as in time lapse video.
The night rolls up

its garage door. I leave
having gained

nothing. At least
I'm alone, a tempest

of styrofoam chewed
from the rim of my cup.

EXERCISE IN DEFLECTION or
"When you left, I felt a sense of loss

and couldn't sleep," you told me at 3, or 5 am,
from a cabin somewhere in Manitoba.
I wondered about your particulars:

the forecast, for one,
and if one day you might call, and more importantly
what that might be called.

I wondered about the river, there,
looked out at the Saint John
and pretended it was somewhere else.

It was easy to wonder about anything then,
before we developed our own particulars:
is September so far away? And so on.

From my window it's hard to believe
the river is really there. It's just I've never had
been so close before.

I looked out one morning and it was a brand new shade;
something optimistic, or at least a nostalgia
that I'd neglected to project onto it before.

By the time I reached the edge, the water was different,
another shade, no matter how much
it'd seemed to stand still from a distance.

That is not a metaphor about the distance.

When a new shade of blue was discovered
at Oregon State University, they didn't have the technology
to print it and they printed it anyway,

or, well, an approximation of it.
That has as little or as much to do with
the river as can be determined

from any approximation.
Anyway it is not that kind of blue
and I've become exhausted by inaccuracy.

You hate when I start and don't finish
a thought: it's the fact that the shade is described as
"near-perfect and discovered by accident"...

That *is* a metaphor about the distance.

Studies say that living near water
promotes mental health
and peace of mind. So—

I walk to the pedestrian bridge each day,
stop halfway and forget about the water,
having ambient feelings of romance toward my iPhone.

Who said the thing about re-entering the river,
that the river and the person entering both become changed?
I worry giving credit where it is due

forfeits the charm of the allusion.
Besides, in one way it's only two hours' difference.
In another way it's 5h45.

It was Heraclitus and I got it wrong,
he didn't mean what I meant.
No, you can't necessarily enter the same river twice,

they continue to be different rivers,
but I continue to sit by the side
performing a particular petal-plucking ritual.

I wanted to do this like W.C.W.
(keep it brief, I mean...)
to maintain my claim to a penchant for complication,

put simply, and nice.
How much simpler could I put it:
It feels like

18 and overcast, what about over there?

AND SO I DO

I've gone to work at the iron
Straightening out my difficulties

A laugh downstairs,
I repeat the joke

Up here, hiding
from my own engagement party

Oh how many ways
Must I be

Before I've rounded out
A ring

Of myself

The other woman *is* beautiful
And not going anywhere

None of them are
Imagine

A world of just myself,
And those who admire my talents.

It just wouldn't do

WE WERE ON THE ST. CROIX

for a moment.

And yes, I wondered:
really?

It was the strangest thing:
I read a story you sent me
and thought about

holding you in a cabin
in Pine Cove.

But the words were all just about
geography and the sound of
a branch snapping under
your boot.

GOODBYE TO NEW YORK

I said goodbye to New York
this past October. The dream of it, that is.
Travelled to London (Ontario) and settled in for a month
before ending up in Fredericton.

I had a room of my own
and a column. Just like

Carrie Bradshaw!
No, it's Virginia, I think, and anyway
we similarly starve.

A reader suggested I become a counselor to the lonely.
What a strange idea.

His wife, whom he now mourns only in fragments,
said

> "The issue is that this is the best you can do,"
> He said, describing his current work,
> the work of grieving in smaller and smaller doses.
>
> He said you don't forget, you just
> think more and more of other things, too.

4

WOOF

The exposure therapist says he understands me:
at fifteen he was attacked by a dog.

He, too, hoarded small anxieties. He, too,
remained indoors. He hung a muzzle

from his bedroom doorknob, slotted his keys
between his fingers and made a fist.

In mid-life, he has learned to let go.
We speak over the phone and I imagine him

perfect, or covered in scars.
It depends on how my day is going.

I describe the sofa to him in great detail:
it is stuffed with down. Ornate, white, and firm.

It is where my mother died. Not exactly
where my mother died, but dying

can take time. He asks for more.
Says he cannot picture it, but almost.

What do you like so much
about it? he says. Though he knows

it is not about the sofa,
as it was not about the dog.

He's never heard of Joan Didion
when I tell him she kept

her dead husband's shirts in her closet,
in case he needed them again.

The exposure therapist makes me un-right
a painting of a naked woman, soft and asleep.

For forty minutes I look at the thing, crooked,
and then we say goodbye.

When I vomit during a session he says:
good, some people think their heads

are going to explode. When he was fifteen
they let him stand in the doorway

while they injected a substance into the dog
that did it. This, he says, is when he first

fell in love with exposure and response
prevention. He says unlike him,

I never got the closure of seeing the body,
or of seeing the body go into the ground.

He tells me he's forgiven himself.
He forgives me too, even if I don't.

For what? I ask. The exposure therapist
has two dogs who bark in the background

of our calls. See? he says. I'm not lying
about this stuff. He makes me poke a pin

through a sofa cushion. He makes me rip up
my mother's journals, break her plates

over my knee. He says I shatter glass
with a sense of timid preservation.

He says I clean up my messes too soon
after our calls. He is insatiable,

knowing what he knows about the sofa.
You do this, he says, and you won't need me

anymore. The pills didn't work
and neither did the talking and the talking

and the talking. I have to drag the sofa
to the curb. This is the bitter bread of failure.

But, I ask him, what if I'm not looking
when they come to take it away?

HOPING
Poem written by AI in response to poem written by Fawn Parker

My father meets me at the door
to tell me he and John
had a meeting.
That's my mother's brother.

He walks around the house
from room to room in a daze,
trying to decide what to do
and where to do it.

They talked it over,
tried to understand the situation,
as always, together.
The decisions, the will, the event.

And I reply:
Is this what you guys do?

Get together to talk
like lawyers?
Ask other people
for other people's opinions?

I call John, my mother's brother,
to hear his disembodied voice.
I can hear her softly saying his name.

And I break down,
my cheek pressed to the
receiver.

Is it a badge of honor
to communicate something
to someone to whom
you have no relationship?

Or a sign of emotional
absence? No one will just
listen to the document
due to its coldness.

He is going on:

How does it make you feel
to be treated like you're part
of a study
being watched
with unprecedented intensity

by our government,
as though your private conversations
have suddenly become
the most important story?

I love you, John, I say
but my mouth is silent,
as always, hoping

he understands.

ASSHOLE

Funny how I am so bold as to sit before Bliss

to approach the great line of spruces
in the burial ground on Forest Hill.

A dead orange ring of needles on my door.

It reminds me of the way that they cook in the sun
in the cemetery where I run from corner to corner.

It is the eve of launching myself out
and into something that will not know my name,

I've come again to observe but not address
the stillness, the changing hue, the river

all the way over there,
dark and prophetic.

August! You come so slow,
I cannot wait for you to end.

Twice already I sinned by beckoning to them.
Dare I invoke their soldierly arrangement?

Meaningless, now, anachronistic in contemporary moment.

Maximalistic, mouth on own tail.
I reek of thesaurus.

So be it—on and on about the trees.
Finally, I am an asshole.

I placed the A, considered, no—
apostle?

BLUFF CHARGE

Oh, to drop keys in swing-bowl!
Chaperoned and shrouded in shrapnel
and chardonnay. Shined like brogue,
polished and perforated, knot tied
over tongue. Oh, to be young and dream
of Venus. To embrace the limb of the city—
its scurrying organ, pierced with sudden
steel. The muscle ripped from water
by its lip, skins stomped in buckets,
poison in brain. Oh, to be carnivorous.
Feed on sin, shriveling in the rectory.
White wine and oysters, pearl beneath lid,
gun in paper bag, booze behind trap door,
father not father, then father again.
To pray at base of phallic stem of glass,
horseradish red wine vinegar parmesan
white wine and oysters. Yonically
architectured vulvular offering.
Patient… is Aphrodite in the room
with us right now? In mo(u)rning, scrape
ancient breakfast from his dish. Suckle
on bruise of hangover, holy light of sun.
Skulk-like, slink to marital mattress.
Sink into sea, shrink into shell. Wake,
clenched as salted leech, puckered in divet
on wrong side of bed. Oh, river through city.
Treated water reeking of ejaculate.
Throbbing lighthouse of husband!
Beam upward through skyline. Are we not
siren, but mother? Having sufficiently
shirked seduction? Deflating in the rectory,
releasing some clotted criminal. They call

her miscarriage, doctor and litmus. Wily,
them—to name a thing not meant to be.
Slumped over podium, she with soft shell,
inferior to consistent supply. Tailed things.
Amphibian, Darwinian in progression,
suspended in sickly slime. Many in number
and potent. She's grown only to meet some
sad potential: risen from scalloped shard,
dry-egged and Mary-blue. Metastasized
and failingly therapied. And they say she's the one
who carries the empty briefcase like it's not empty.

HORESEMAN'S FIRST RODEO

I, workhorse

once rode muscular

back of beast

round field

sans harness

paid cash

for equestrian promise

of anachronistic aim

tendon gliding over vertebrae

satisfied

closed shop

hauled ass

to water

drank with ease:

evidence of horse

without horse instinct

chosen incorrectly

on impulse

misplaced bet

besides

mastery only ever

depressed a person

sitting idly

on spangled saddle

SICKLEBILL ABANDONS

Post-prime, a womb-image,
reversed uterus
fanned in horizontal
inflorescence:
the bird of paradise
grows exclusively this way
co-inhabited
counter-queened
an all-yellow
all-hormone
large-measuring monarch,
a petalled thing
sips from spathe
pollinates post-pollination,
orobourosly
with gold-costumed
feet, plumage variation
gives rise to passions
with which to distract,
to regard as souvenirs
...anomalies... ?
gratitude turned over
to de-preserve
to be plucked,
her mournful noises
not quite language
unable to
        'aaak?'
properly, with right
grammar, ease
of communication
flapping wingbeats

across dark hallways
composing texts
hoarding letters
in the den of feeling
with memories
of one who dined
on the silk of her body
and then migrated
de-imagined her children
her allure
the damp basket of her nest
the sweetness of limbs
and feathers
gone heavy, limp
and fluttering
in memory of a wing's rage.

THURSDAY,

and you wring
out the washcloth.

Orange October
morning.
Stripped rotting wood.

See the simple object anew:
the mug,
perched on the railing.

I know
through breakfast
I am leaving you.

I watch out the window,
practicing—
in here, without you.

You are arched
in your way,
over the porch.

The brush,
dragged through primer,
sheds a single bristle.

I dump my coffee
over your plates,
and leave them.

Tomorrow,
a curtain draws
over the front door.

THURSDAY, AGAIN

and I wring
out my hair.

Shiver in my
embarrassing form,
robed

in terry and product
stench.
Everything

out the window
is boring.
What am I to do

while you are away,
just stand
in this stupid room?

Talk politics
with our friends?
Or think?

I haven't called,
like we said.
I've been busy

looking
at the heavy egg
of "goodnight"—

timeless,
unbroken,
and oblong.

At breakfast
I hesitate. A bloodspot
in the yolk.

I starve
for sport.
Make romance

out of lack,
miss
and long.

I crack
and it all
opens:

home, the sky,
my stupid,
boring heart.

How cruel—
you, banished,
and I allow the threat of myself.

A COVER OVER EVERYTHING

The first snowfall came in the night,
a cover over everything.
Depressing the posture of the trees
I awoke impatiently to the grief
and novelty in our differences
on the "world clock" and the weather.
I was shoveling when you texted me
you slept "fitfully." I'd rushed inside
to tell you that a bird fell out of the sky
and landed in the mouth of my shovel
but forgot when I reached my desk,
agreeing dishonestly that I'd also barely
slept. In fact the night disappeared
in the flash of dream. This always happens:
boarding for Toronto, I remember my fear
of flying too late. Disappointed, you refuse
to come with me, to beg the pilot to stop.
The plane accelerates, banks left
and I wake, the heaviness of my body
in take-off no more than the duvet.
Heavy and white and feathered. I shed
the mess of bedding and went outside
in your sweater and boots, worked at the snow
until the bird fell. I figured the thing
was dead, or if not would somehow disappear
on its own. I coudn't stand the thought
of trying and failing to save it.

ACKNOWLEDGEMENTS

Thank you first and foremost to Jim Johnstone for the years of support. Thank you to Professor Triny Finlay and my classmates in the UNB graduate poetry workshop (Tommy Duggan, Rosie Leggott, Jamie Kitts), to my good friend and collaborator Joshua Chris Bouchard, to Elliot Burns, Mary Germaine, Ali Pinkney, Quinn Mason, Sophie McCreesh, Joe MacNeil, Cody Caetano, Jack Christie, Jake Morrow, Jasmine Vatuloka, and the writing communities in Toronto, Montreal, and Fredericton. Thank you to my father and my aunt Beth, and to my mother for our too-brief time together.

Thanks to the editors of the following publications where poems in *Soft Inheritance* previous appeared;

Echolocation: "In the Documentary About the Entire World"

The Puritan: "Golden Rays of Chemo"

Vallum: "1986, The Fields Company of Chicago"

CAROUSEL: "Woof"

Literary Review of Canada: "Sicklebill Abandons"

Several poems also appeared in the chapbook *Weak Spot* (Anstruther Press, 2018).

PHOTO: STEPH MARTYNIUK

Fawn Parker is the author of *Set-Point* (ARP Books), *Dumb-Show* (ARP Books), *What We Both Know* (McClelland & Stewart), and the forthcoming auto-memoir *Hi, it's me* (McClelland & Stewart). Her novel *What We Both Know* was nominated for the 2022 Giller Prize and her essay "The Prescription" was nominated for a 2023 National Magazine Award. Short fiction and poetry have appeared in *The Walrus*, *Maisonneuve*, and *Literary Review of Canada*. Fawn lives in Fredericton and is a PhD student in Creative Writing at the University of New Brunswick.